# Little Princess

## GUEST BOOK

### It's a GIRL

_____

_____

# Little Princess

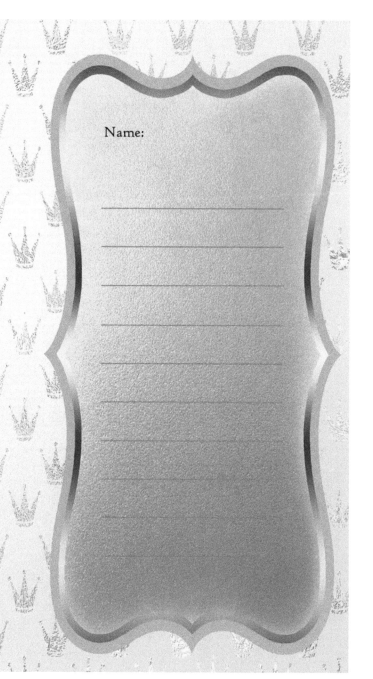

Name:

Little Princess

Name:

# Little Princess

Name:

_____

_____

_____

_____

_____

_____

_____

_____

Little

Princess

Name:

_____

_____

_____

_____

_____

_____

_____

_____

# Little Princess

Name:

_____

_____

_____

_____

_____

_____

_____

_____

_____

*Little Princess*

Name:

_____

_____

_____

_____

_____

_____

_____

_____

Little
Princess

Name:

_____

_____

_____

_____

_____

# Little Princess

Name:

_____

_____

_____

_____

_____

_____

_____

_____

Little

Princess

Name:

# Little Princess

Name:

_____

_____

_____

_____

_____

_____

Little

Princess

Name:

# Little Princess

Name:

_____

_____

_____

_____

_____

_____

_____

_____

Little

Princess

Name:

# Little Princess

Name:

_____

_____

_____

_____

_____

_____

_____

Little

Princess

Name:

_____

_____

_____

_____

_____

_____

_____

_____

_____

_____

_____

# Little Princess

Name:

_____

_____

_____

_____

_____

_____

_____

_____

Little Princess

Name:

_____

_____

_____

_____

_____

_____

_____

_____

# Little Princess

Name:

_____

_____

_____

_____

_____

_____

_____

_____

Little Princess

Name:

_____

_____

_____

_____

_____

_____

_____

# Little Princess

Name:

_____

_____

_____

_____

_____

_____

_____

Little

Princess

Name:

_____

_____

_____

_____

_____

_____

_____

_____

Little Princess

Name:

*Little*

*Princess*

Name:

_____

_____

_____

_____

_____

_____

_____

# Little Princess

Name:

_____

_____

_____

_____

_____

_____

_____

_____

_____

# Little Princess

Name:

_____

_____

_____

_____

_____

_____

_____

_____

Little

Princess

Name:

Little Princess

Name:

# Little Princess

Name:

_____

_____

_____

_____

_____

# Little Princess

Name:

_____

_____

_____

_____

_____

_____

_____

Little Princess

Name:

Little
Princess

Name:

# Little Princess

**Name:**

_____

_____

_____

_____

_____

_____

_____

Little Princess

Name:
_____
_____
_____
_____
_____
_____
_____

*Little*

*Princess*

Name:

_____

_____

_____

_____

_____

_____

_____

_____

_____

_____

Little

Princess

Name:

_____

_____

_____

_____

_____

_____

_____

# Little Princess

**Name:**

_____

_____

_____

_____

_____

_____

_____

Little Princess

Name:

Little Princess

Name:

_____

_____

_____

# Little Princess

Name:

_____

_____

_____

_____

_____

_____

_____

_____

_____

# Little Princess

**Name:**

_____

_____

_____

_____

_____

Little

Princess

Name:

Little Princess

Name:

# Little Princess

Name:

_____

_____

_____

_____

_____

_____

_____

_____

# Little Princess

Name:

_____

_____

_____

_____

_____

_____

Little Princess

Name:

_____
_____
_____
_____
_____
_____
_____
_____

# Little Princess

Name:

_____

_____

_____

_____

_____

_____

_____

_____

Little Princess

Name:

_____

_____

_____

_____

_____

_____

_____

_____

*Little*

*Princess*

Name:

_____

_____

_____

_____

_____

_____

Little Princess

Name:

_____

_____

_____

_____

_____

_____

_____

_____

Little
Princess

Name:

*Little*

*Princess*

Name:

_____

_____

_____

_____

_____

_____

_____

# Little Princess

Name:

_____

_____

_____

_____

_____

_____

_____

Little Princess

Name:

Little

Princess

Name:

*Little*
*Princess*

Name:

_____

_____

_____

_____

_____

_____

_____

_____

_____

*Little Princess*

Name:

_____

_____

_____

_____

_____

_____

_____

_____

# Little Princess

Name:

_____

_____

_____

_____

_____

_____

_____

_____

Little

Princess

Name:

_____

Little

Princess

Name:

_____

_____

_____

_____

_____

_____

_____

_____

# Little Princess

Name:

_____

_____

_____

_____

_____

Little Princess

Name:

# Little Princess

Name:

Little

Princess

Name:

# Little Princess

Name:

_____

_____

_____

_____

_____

_____

_____

_____

Little Princess

Name:

Little
Princess

Name:

Little Princess

Name:

# Little Princess

Name:

_____

_____

_____

_____

_____

_____

*Little Princess*

Name:

_____

_____

_____

_____

_____

_____

_____

_____

_____

Little
Princess

Name:

*Little*

*Princess*

Name:

# Little Princess

Name:

_____

_____

_____

_____

_____

_____

_____

*Little Princess*

Name:

_____

_____

_____

_____

_____

_____

_____

_____

_____

Little

Princess

Name:

Little Princess

Name:

# Little Princess

Name:

_____

_____

_____

_____

_____

_____

_____

_____

_____

*Little*

*Princess*

Name:

_____

_____

_____

_____

_____

_____

_____

_____

_____

Little
Princess

Name:

# Little Princess

Name:

_____

_____

_____

_____

_____

_____

_____

_____

# Little Princess

**Name:**

_____

_____

_____

_____

_____

_____

# Little Princess

Name:

Little Princess

Name:

## Little Princess

Name:

_____

_____

_____

_____

_____

_____

_____

# Little Princess

Name:

# Little Princess

Name:

_____

_____

_____

_____

_____

_____

_____

_____

Little
Princess

Name:

# Little Princess

Name:

# Little Princess

Name:
_____
_____
_____
_____
_____
_____
_____
_____

Little Princess

Name:

# Little Princess

Name:

_____

_____

_____

_____

_____

Little Princess

Name:

# Little Princess

Name:

_____

_____

_____

_____

_____

_____

_____

*Little Princess*

Name:

_____

_____

_____

_____

_____

_____

_____

_____

Little

Princess

Name:

# Little Princess

Name:

_____

_____

_____

_____

_____

_____

_____

_____

_____

# Little Princess

Name:

_____

_____

_____

_____

_____

_____

_____

_____

_____

*Little Princess*

Name:

_____

_____

_____

_____

_____

_____

_____

_____

_____

# Little Princess

Name:

_____

_____

_____

_____

_____

_____

_____

_____

*Little Princess*

Name:

_____

_____

_____

_____

_____

_____

_____

*Little*

*Princess*

Name:

_____

_____

_____

_____

_____

_____

_____

_____

_____

_____

# Little PRINCESS

*Thank you!*

*We hope your experience was awesome and we can't wait to see you again soon.*

*As a small company, your feedback is very important to us.*

*Please let as know how you like our book at:*

*monicagopublish20@yahoo.com*

CPSIA information can be obtained
at www.ICGtesting.com
Printed in the USA
BVHW010713270621
610445BV00020B/162